M000019658

Disappointed But Not Disillusioned

SEXUAL ABUSE, DIVORCE, LOSS, AND
ROMANS 8:28

Debbie Dickens Morgan

TRILOGY CHRISTIAN PUBLISHERS
TUSTIN, CA

Trilogy Christian Publishers
A Wholly Owned Subsidiary of Trinity Broadcasting Network
2442 Michelle Drive
Tustin, CA 92780

Copyright © 2021 by Debbie Dickens Morgan

Scripture quotations marked AMP are taken from the Amplified® Bible (AMP), Copyright © 2015 by The Lockman Foundation. Used by permission. www.Lockman.org.

Scripture quotations marked NIV are taken from the Holy Bible, New International Version®, NIV®. Copyright © 1973, 1978, 1984, 2011 by Biblica, Inc.TM Used by permission of Zondervan. All rights reserved worldwide. www.zondervan.com. The "NIV" and "New International Version" are trademarks registered in the United States Patent and Trademark Office by Biblica, Inc.TM

Scripture quotations marked KJV are taken from the King James Version of the Bible. Public domain.

Scripture quotations marked HCSB are taken from the Holman Christian Standard Bible®, Used by Permission HCSB © 1999, 2000, 2002, 2003, 2009 Holman Bible Publishers. Holman Christian Standard Bible®, Holman CSB®, and HCSB® are federally registered trademarks of Holman Bible Publishers.

Scripture quotations marked NKJV are taken from the New King James Version®. Copyright © 1982 by Thomas Nelson. Used by permission. All rights reserved.

Scripture quotations marked GNT are taken from the Good News Translation® (Today's English Version, Second Edition). Copyright © 1982 American Bible Society. All rights reserved.

Scripture quotations marked ISV are taken from the International Standard Version® The Holy Bible: International Standard Version. Release 2.0, Build 2015.02.09. Copyright © 1995-2014 by ISV Foundation. ALL RIGHTS RESERVED INTERNATIONALLY. Used by permission of Davidson Press, LLC.

No part of this book may be reproduced, stored in a retrieval system, or transmitted by any means without written permission from the author.

All rights reserved, including the right to reproduce this book or portions thereof in any form whatsoever.

For information, address Trilogy Christian Publishing

Rights Department, 2442 Michelle Drive, Tustin, Ca 92780.

Trilogy Christian Publishing/ TBN and colophon are trademarks of Trinity Broadcasting Network.

For information about special discounts for bulk purchases, please contact Trilogy Christian Publishing.

Manufactured in the United States of America

Trilogy Disclaimer: The views and content expressed in this book are those of the author and may not necessarily reflect the views and doctrine of Trilogy Christian Publishing or the Trinity Broadcasting Network.

10 9 8 7 6 5 4 3 2 1

Library of Congress Cataloging-in-Publication Data is available.

ISBN 978-1-63769-188-5

ISBN 978-1-63769-189-2 (ebook)

Contents

Dedication

This book is dedicated to Leighton, Bennett, Remy, and Baylor. May you always be willing to take your disappointments to your heavenly Father.

Acknowledgements

This book was a labor of love that came to be published with the help and prayers of several individuals.

I want to thank the people at TBN publishing for believing in this message and allowing me to publish it,

The many friends and family who have prayed and proofread many chapters for me,

My son and daughter for allowing me to share our story, and my beautiful daughter-in-law for all the computer help and prayers,

My Lord and Savior Jesus Christ (You are the best person to take disappointment to),

And last, but not least: my beautiful grandchildren, Leighton, Bennett, Remy, and Baylor. You are Grammy's "happily ever after!"

And we know [with great confidence] that God [who is deeply concerned about us] causes all things to work together [as a plan] for good for those who love God, to those who are called according to His plan and purpose.

Romans 8:28 (AMP)

Introduction

Disappointed: *adjective*, "defeated in expectation or hope."

Disillusioned: *adjective*, "having lost faith or trust in something formerly regarded as good or valuable."

We have all faced disappointment. It is not fun, but usually not fatal. Disillusionment, however, is a slippery slope that can be fatal. It is my hope that my readers will be encouraged to not let disappointment turn to disillusion.

Today, I told my Sunday school class that I was writing a book. Wow—I guess I'm "all in" now and had better follow through on this thing. I have considered writing a book for a little over fifteen years now, but I was never sure it was a task I could take on and complete. It seemed like an impossibility for me. I was busy, you know—surviving, raising broken teens, working to pay bills, and dating.... or something like it. I was busy keeping my chin up and putting on my "Romans 8:28" face for my friends at church to see. For those of you who are not familiar with the verse, it states that God causes all things believers go through to be used for good and for God's glory.

Please don't get me wrong; I was not trying to be fake or make myself look like a super-Christian. My friends and family will tell you that I am bluntly honest, to a fault sometimes. I am very open and transparent. My goal in putting on this brave face was to do just what the verse says: to give God the glory; to believe that good would come at some point from all of the pain and sorrow my family had gone through. I think in some strange way, I was trying to cover for God.

This situation does not look good for His reputation, right? To believe that a God we trust and count on would allow an innocent child to be tormented and sexually abused by her earthly father is disgusting, not tolerable. A father who was a deacon in the church, a father who read the Bible and prayed with his kids, no less. This husband whom I loved very much, prayed for and believed was God's will for my life as a mate. To think he could commit such vile acts with a child and then crawl in bed with me and tell me how much he loved me... It's mind-blowing, and it looks like God was out taking a nap those days, right?

However, to believe that I serve and love a God whose ways are much higher than mine and who will turn even this horrific abuse into "something" good is a thought that I can not only tolerate, but even celebrate. I remember reading this verse in the Bible: "I remain confident of this: I will see the goodness of the Lord in the land of the living. Wait for the Lord; be strong and take heart and wait for the Lord." This is found in the book of Psalms, verses 27:13-14 (NIV). I took this to mean that in my earthly lifetime, I would see the goodness of the Lord, and I can honestly say at this writing that I have seen much of the goodness of God. But I am skipping ahead, aren't I?

For so many years, I wanted to just be done with this topic. I mean, I did the hard stuff: divorced the perpetrator, sought counseling for the victim (who cried), cried much more, and watched the struggle of my sweet child trying to process the "un-processable." I got it. It was going to take years; it was going to hurt. I was going to need to seek help for my child with no health insurance. I was going to need to make sure my other child got the help he needed to heal and deal with the loss of his father. I was going to go from being a stay-at-home mom to a single mom on food stamps looking for any job I could get in the middle of winter living in a tourist town. The one person I would turn to in a crisis—my best friend and husband—was the one who caused it all.

This recovery was not going to be easy or pretty. It was, after all, a huge family crisis. To go from loving your husband one day to acknowledging he is now a criminal is not easy by any stretch of the imagination. Then, to mentally process what your child has gone through is mind-blowing. How bad was it? How long did it go on? Where did it take place? Why didn't she tell me? Why didn't I catch him? These are some of the many questions I had to process. I was even willing to mentor some younger girls who were dealing with sexual abuse on a college campus I worked at several years later. The thought of writing a book about it was not on my list of reasonable things to be asked to do by the Lord. Don't get me wrong: I am not saying that the Lord sent me this postcard that said, "Write the book." It was just that every time over the years when I would pray or look for direction in my life, I felt the prompting of God to write this book.

This abuse had brought a level of pain and misery and fallout for my family that I could not put into a million books, not to mention my sweet in-laws. I was very close to them. Watching them try to walk this tightrope of loving the kids and me while still loving and trying to help the perpetrator was difficult on all of us. Those of you reading this right now who are living through the aftermath or currently suffering from the pain of sexual abuse know what I am talking about. Please know I am praying for you as this book gets published.

This issue is all over the church today. I was told in my own home church it is really not even much of a shock anymore to be dealing with a sexual offender in the church. There is a procedure, a manual, a way to "best deal with" and hold a sex offender accountable in the church body. My church was not making light of it; they were just stating the reality that is now a common situation having to be dealt with.

There is no neat, pretty bow to wrap this subject up in. If I had written my life's story, it would have had a much different outcome. I think most of us who have had a few years tucked under our belt could say the same. After this came several other disappointments: losses of jobs, depression, suicidal thoughts, and dealing with a divorce, to name a few. I am certain I am not the only one who has dealt with these issues.

My life's story would have been something like this had I written it: "Godly woman saves her purity for her husband, husband messes up.... big time. Woman deals, child heals.... Prince Charming comes along a few reasonable years later. He loves godly woman and becomes a godly father to her two broken teenagers, and they all live happily ever after!" This was not my journey at all. Seventeen years into this story, we are not living anything close to the way I would have written our story. Despite this reality, I have seen God do miracles with our messy story. It doesn't make it all okay, but it has brought us healing and purpose.

I know I am not alone here. The details are different, but disappointment is so common and so much a part of all of our stories. Why do we find this so surprising? Why are these disappointments so shocking to us? Jesus told us plain and simple in John 16:33 (KJV): in this world, you will have trouble, "But be of good cheer; I have overcome the world." This scripture can't be taken in too many ways. It's not a mysterious parable to be figured out. If you are in this world—which pretty much covers anyone reading this book—you will have trouble.

I am learning that disappointments are normal in a fallen world; part of life on this earth. I am starting to not be surprised or outraged when they come. Don't get me wrong, they are still very painful, but when I realize they are a part of my journey, it takes some of the sting out. I am learning to view trials as like having a personal trainer. When we are going through the pain and testing, the Lord is right there in it with us. Just like my trainer at the gym, he stands beside me, assisting me with the weights or counting the squats. It's not just that trials like squats are good for us... I mean, who wants to hear that? It's that my trainer is there with me during the workout. He even knows when to tell me to rest and go get a drink (thanks Jordan)!

Isn't that the helpful part: knowing that God is our trainer? He is training us for something bigger and better during our times of deep sorrow and disappointment. We know and believe that He is not only watching and guiding us, but that He is right there beside us, adjusting the weights and reminding us to take a drink when our souls are parched and thirsty from the workout of this life.

I am by no means saying that God causes sexual abuse or divorce; His heart breaks when these things happen, as ours will, too. It reminds me of the story of Joseph in the Bible. This guy had his share of disappointments: left for dead by his brothers, sold into slavery, accused of adultery, thrown into prison, and forgotten by those he had helped. His amazing story is found in the book of Genesis. The lesson I get from this story is that God was always with him. The Bible says it over and over. He went to jail, but God was with him; he was falsely accused, but God was with him. Over and over, it shows God was being kind to him, even though at the moment he wasn't being delivered from his trial.

The end of his story shows the "Romans 8:28" belief for sure! In Genesis 50:20, Joseph tells his brothers that what they did to him they meant for evil, but God meant it for good. It wasn't that God was okay with the horrible way Joseph was treated. God did not cause the bad behavior, but he turned it around and let it lead to something very good. Joseph was able to save many lives during a famine because of the position he had acquired while in Egypt. God also blessed him on a personal level. He reconciled with his brothers and was given children of his own. He was able to move his father and all his family to Egypt, and they were given a very good home.

I finally wrote this book not to embarrass anyone or shame them. That includes the perpetrator. My former husband has served his long prison sentence, and his future is between him and God now. I want no contact with him, but I also want to leave him in God's hands and not hold on to bitterness. When we remain bitter and angry at the person or persons who have wronged us, we only further the damage done to our hearts. Forgiveness is not an easy process, but for our own sakes, we need to work through that and be able to move on at the appropriate time. I don't know who said this, but most of us know the old saying that "bitterness causes more damage in the vessel in which it is stored than the vessel on which it is poured." I wish I would have come up with that saying, it's so good!

There is a lot of shame in sexual abuse and in many of the other disappointments I share in these pages. Writing a book that involves your family members is risky. For so many years, I have felt the pull to share our story in the hope of encouraging and helping others. The problem with many of these topics is that I am not the only victim—in fact, I'm not even the main victim in the sexual abuse story. I had to wait many years for the right time and the go-ahead from my kids. We have had time to heal and to watch God do some amazing things with our story. I had to come to grips with all the ugly stuff being "put out there." What if people are unkind to my loved ones on the internet? No doubt, there will be lots of opinions on what I am about the share.

The purpose of this book is to point to the only One who can deliver us from the sting of sexual abuse and other deep disappointments. I have learned that there is nothing God can't deliver us from and use for the good of others. I know that is a bold statement, but I say it out of much experience. I desire to shed light on the subject and help all of us know how to minister to those who are victims of abuse and other disappointments. When we keep our lessons in the dark and out of sight, it is a waste, in my opinion. I want to show off the God who has delivered this broken and hurting family (not overnight, but it did come); the God who has walked me through my own sexual abuse as a child at the hand of a babysitter and many other disappointments—some self-inflicted and some at the hands of others—and through bankruptcy, divorce, job losses, and suicidal thoughts.

These disappointments have shaped me and given me an empathy for others that I thank God for. At the time, I didn't really care if what I was going through would help others, but now, I see all of the struggles in a different light. I have had the strange gift of getting to know Jesus in His sufferings—not that mine are anywhere close to His. So far, I have not been nailed to a cross!

God does not need a PR person. His character and Word are solid. I just want to encourage others and give real-life proof that He is faithful. I have argued with Him, questioned His methods, and even doubted many times. I believe He welcomed all of this. He is relational to the core, and relationships are messy. I am not advocating that we doubt God, but let's be honest: don't we all have that doubt at times of disappointments and struggle?

What God did for people in the Bible, He can do for you. Some promises in the Bible are conditional, like "trust in the Lord with all your heart and He will make your paths straight." The condition is for us to trust Him, the promise is that He will guide us. This promise is found in Psalms 37:4. There are some promises in the Bible that are promises with no conditions attached.

The promise in Hebrews that He will never leave nor forsake us is one of many such promises.

When we go to God and are honest with our prayers and disappointments, He hears us and He works with us to resolve the issue. Maybe He takes away the problem, or maybe He chooses to give strength and walk right through the battle with us for reasons we don't usually understand at the time. Most of us can call to mind someone who has lost a child or has a health crisis and still is a person of joy. We can also think of others with similar circumstances who are bitter. What is the difference? How can this be? We will explore this in the pages to come.

These are dark issues that so many are struggling with. From one ruptured and redeemed soul to another, your disappointments are not the final chapter of your amazing story! I know if you are picking up this book, you must be hurting or know someone who is… or you are one my friends or family members who promised to buy a copy! Whichever the case, you are in great company! There is story after story in God's Word about people who faced huge disappointments. Let's unpack some of these together. If you are not a Christian, or not even sure what that means, please don't put the book down. Listen to the stories of real people who faced real hurts and turned to a real God. You were created by Him and He loves you. Even as I type that sentence, I squirm a bit. I never want to present a "Pollyanna" type of attitude, but I do believe that sentence with all my heart. God does love you. Hang in there with me, and let's look at this concept.

CHAPTER 1

The Disappointment of Sexual Abuse

The Disappointment: Sexual abuse.

The Disillusion: "I am forever dirty, damaged, and will never recover from being a victim of sexual abuse."

As long as I live, I will never forget the day of December 22, 2002. It was cold and snowing where we lived. My family loves the snow. We live in southwest Missouri and we get more ice than snow. I had just returned from a Caribbean cruise with my elderly mother. I had been able to get away without the kids for a week and just relax and rest. Looking back now, I see the grace of God in that week away. I would need the strength, for the very next day, our lives imploded. Life was good, and I was excited to be doing some Christmas shopping with my beautiful daughter. She was my shopping buddy! She was in her sophomore year of high school, making good grades and on the cheerleading squad. She was active in her youth group at our church and it looked like her life thus far was pretty rosy. There was absolutely no indication of the nightmare she was living.

She was driving her cute little car we bought her when she turned sixteen and I was in the passenger seat. We were just visiting like moms and daughters do when she said these words: "I need to tell you something, but it is going to ruin your entire life!" Her sweet little teenage face was serious and scared, and her eyes were filling up with tears. I remember processing those words. I had no idea what she needed to tell me, not a clue! I could see that my daughter needed a strong mom at that moment, and I wanted to take whatever burden she was carrying off her shoulders. So, I replied, "Sweetheart, I have no idea what you need to tell me, but my entire life is rooted and grounded in Jesus Christ, and nothing you or anyone else can say could possibly change that. Go ahead and tell me what you need to."

I made some mistakes in how I handled the next few years, but I thank God that at that moment I was able to say and mean what I said. My world did in fact crumble around me, but the foundation was solid and in my faith in God. I am certain that had that not been the case, I would have not survived the next several years.

It rocked me to the core. Do you know that little kids' song that talks about the wise man building his house upon the rock and "the rains came tumbling down?" This principal is found in the book of Matthew 87:24-25. That is how I felt at that moment. The rains started to pour and continued to pour for many years. Most of our lives were washed away, but the foundation stood firm and solid.

Those words I replied with still play in my mind all these years later. They were tested to the fullest! Upon hearing my reply, she went on to tell me that her father had been sexually molesting her for the majority of her young sixteen-year-old life! I vividly remember seeing my life completely crumble down to the foundation, which thank God, was God. It felt just like watching the World Trade Center towers tumble on television the year prior: unreal, numbing, and all reduced to ash. Many years later, just as there is now a beautiful memorial at the World Trade Center site, our life became a beautiful rebuilding.

I asked my daughter to pull the car over. We pulled into a lot that is now our local Chick-Fil-A. I am so glad they tore down the shop that was in that spot on that day, because I don't think I could have been able to drive past it daily these past seventeen years without the raw pain and emotion of that moment coming back.

I'm thankful there is something good there at that place now; something new! I love me some great Chick-Fil-A.

The steps I took next are still so vivid in my head. I asked her to step out of the car, called her father and confirmed the nightmare was indeed true. My school-age son was currently home with his dad and the weather was starting to turn bad. I drove us on to the mall, handed my daughter a $100.00 bill, and told her to go buy whatever she wanted, while I stayed in my car and processed. That seems like a silly way to deal, but at the moment, all I wanted to do was "something" for her! Those were numbing moments, to say the least.

I started making phone calls to my family and then called my husband and told him to get out of our house at once. I realize now how hard that was on our son. He was thirteen at the time and thought his dad was his hero. He watched his dad packing a suitcase and telling him that he was leaving! We had always taught our children that marriage was forever; that we would always work out any difficulties we had and never divorce. I can't imagine how hard that was for him to process. He was so young, and now he was standing in our house all alone, trying to figure out what was happening. I called him several times, but just didn't want to drop all of this on him over the phone. I finally told him to go next door to our neighbor's house and wait until I got home. I called our neighbor and told her I couldn't share all of the details at the moment, but I just needed her to love on my son. She was such a blessing.

As the weather got worse, I wanted to get my daughter back in the car and head home. Of all the days, this one just happened to involve a rare snowstorm. The forty-five or so miles between me and my son was now shut down! I have lived much of my life in this area and I never remember that highway getting completely shut down. I remember I just wanted to get my daughter and my son and crawl into a bunker or something! The world for us had officially just gone mad! My husband was a well-respected pilot and deacon in our church, and quite frankly, my best friend.

I was in a panic to get home. I didn't know who to call or what to do. My mind was in a daze. I called my father and told him the unthinkable news, begging him to somehow get my daughter and myself home. My son called me several times, and I didn't know how to comfort or give him the information he needed to know about what had just happened to his mostly perfect world. I made several calls to my sister-in-law, who was and has always been such a strong and wise person to go to for advice.

The hours, days, months, and years that followed were some of the most horrific moments of our family's lives. I had to deal with the legal issues. I had to go through an investigation to make sure I was not involved in the abuse. I had to file for divorce, find a job in the dead of winter, go through more legal issues, a sentencing, and bankruptcy. It was so much to adjust to financially and emotionally. Well-meaning friends kept asking why we were getting divorced. It was a shock to everyone. I really didn't want to embarrass my in-laws or my daughter. It wasn't something I was ready to share, and yet I had people keep saying to me, "Can't you go to counseling? Are you sure you want to divorce?"

I had to watch my daughter deal with so much pain and illegitimate guilt. In many ways, the pain for her was just starting. Her father had always told her that if she revealed the abuse to anyone that our family would fall apart, and she was led to believe she was responsible for holding it together. She had become so numb during the abuse. So much more than I am including in this book. My heart breaks for anyone currently in a similar situation. The fallout from sexual abuse is staggering. It has so many ripple effects. My in-laws were dealing with the pain and fallout. My parents were trying to find ways to help. Our church stepped in as well with offers of support. I know there are people dealing with abuse who don't have supportive families or good support. I can't imagine what that would be like, because it was difficult enough with support. If this is your situation, I would encourage you to start by finding a trusted friend, family member, or professional counselor that you can trust. Be wise in whom you open up to, but don't try to deal with abuse alone.

I cannot tell this story without also remembering the amazing ways God took care of our broken, bleeding family. Our church, our friends, and our family all stepped up. I dearly love my former in-laws, and even they did a great job of dealing with this. There were so many tears; so many days where I did not want to go on. When I have spoken at different events about this time in our lives, I say it was like my children needing a blood transfusion from me, but I was bleeding to death. My daughter was dealing with so much misplaced guilt. She was angry, scared, and hurting. I was a mess, trying to hold myself and my kids together.

It has taken over a decade to watch that oozing wound heal into a scar. There was good that came of it, but it was at such a great price to my kids and me. The kids are both adults now, with college degrees and beautiful children of their own. My son went through some rough patches, but kept his faith and ended up marrying a beautiful Christian girl. I know that for my son and my daughter, they are better parents for having gone through the blow-up of our family. There were nights when my teenage kids would drag a blanket and a pillow into my room and sleep on the floor of my bedroom. We all were struggling, but we also wanted to be close by, and just the physical presence of all of us being in the same room brought comfort.

My daughter is the bravest human being I know! Most girls who have gone through what she endured at the hands of her father have turned to drugs and suicide. She has grit! Much of what makes her a good mother to her sweet daughter is the determination to give her daughter a better childhood, and she loves her daughter fiercely. Her story is not a sugarcoated-sweet "happily ever after." She has struggled with relationships and with men in the church. Her father used to pray with her after the abuse, and this gave her a sick and twisted view of what a Godly man looks like. She deals with illegitimate guilt. Many children who are abused are given a false belief that they somehow played a part in it. My daughter loved her dad, and it was such a hard thing to finally tell on him. I admire the woman my daughter is. She is brave, raw, and beautiful! She is still my shopping buddy, too.

My son has always had a drive to be a husband and father. This means the world to him. He is both a successful software developer, husband, and father to three beautiful children. Because of his dad going to prison when he was thirteen, he was raised by myself, and to some degree his big sister! I believe this has made him a better husband and father. His beautiful wife of now ten years has often said that she is thankful Jordan was raised by women! She says it has made him more aware of her needs as a wife. I have asked his permission to share a Facebook post he posted the day his father was released from prison. This post means the world to me, and I look at it often:

"Today, I am leaving to pick up my dad from prison, where he's been for nearly the last sixteen years. While I am excited to reconnect with him, I am mostly thankful for all that God has done for me during those years.

I am eternally grateful to my mom for raising me so well under impossible circumstances, and for my sister, who is the strongest person I've ever met. I am lucky to have grown up with them both, and never once did I ever feel a hole of not having a dad around.

If you are a single parent, I can't imagine how hard that must be, but know that you can raise a child just as effectively as two-parent households. Ultimately, the number of parents, mom or dad, doesn't really matter. All that matters is that the one that's there shows up and loves the kids, and then somehow, we turn out okay!

So, thank you, mom, and thank you, Whittier's. Love you both so much!"

To say that God can redeem sexual abuse seems a little trite and cold. Sexual abuse is a violation of one's body, mind, and soul. To even call the horror of sexual abuse a "disappointment" seems to minimize it as well, yet I speak from raw, painful reality. I know in my own life that I let the sting and shame of sexual abuse have way too much power over me for way too long. I not only watched my child go through it, but I myself was a victim of sexual abuse at the hands of a babysitter. For so many years, I held the secret inside and just thought it would fade away when it stopped. The truth is, if this type of wound is not dealt with, it will not heal. Just as a broken arm if not properly set will heal crooked, the wound of sexual abuse needs to be tended to.

I don't think anyone reading this book needs to be informed of the effects or be given the ugly details. There are many good books on the lasting impacts of being victimized in this way. No matter who the perpetrator is, a trusted family member or a total stranger—to be taken advantage of and used for someone's sexual pleasure leaves a lasting scar on your soul. When I first tossed around the idea of writing a book on disappointments, I was not sure I even wanted to include our story of sexual abuse. I mean, Lord knows there are plenty of other disappointments I have to write about. I sure am not lacking for material about painful, disappointing events in my life.

I am certain that the subject of sexual abuse and how our Lord wants to redeem even this pain needs to be shared, and shared loudly! It became an overwhelming certainty that this subject was to be written about in my book. Timing is a funny thing. As I write these words, my former husband, the perpetrator of the abuse on my family member, is about to wind up his prison sentence and be released. He has served a long and hard prison sentence—one that he fully deserved. I was teaching in my Sunday school class last week and this topic was a part of my lesson.

In the Old Testament book of Nehemiah, there is a story about the children of Israel returning home from exile. They had been carried away to a foreign land for seventy years due to their continued disobedience to God's laws. When they returned, they were gathered together as a nation, and the book of the law was read out loud to them. These would have been the laws that were given to Moses on Mt. Sinai. There was a whole generation that had never been taught about the law and God's rules for keeping them out of captivity. When these laws were read out loud and the people were brought face to face with their sin, they wept loudly. I had been told by family members that my former husband was weeping a lot and that he had been going through the MOSOP program—this is the Missouri Sexual Offender Program. Sexual offenders go through this program when they are about to be released. I can only hope his weeping was a result of getting a look at what he has put his child and our family through.

After teaching this lesson, I had a precious lady in her late sixties come up to me and ask to speak with me in private. I knew right away this was another person who had been a victim of sexual abuse. My friend told me her story of how she was sexually abused by a family member at a very young age. This alone would have been bad enough, but when she went to a parent to cry for help, she was discounted and never given the help she needed. She continued to be abused and was voiceless to cry out for help. When a child comes to a trusted adult with a story of abuse, they need to be heard and taken seriously. Kids can't make something that horrible up! I asked her if she had ever sought out counseling, and she said no.

I believe part of what adds to the pain of sexual abuse is the belief that there is no one we can turn to for help. The lie that somehow, we are at fault. Just yesterday, another friend of mine confided in me that she had been a victim of sexual abuse and she was afraid it might somehow stop her from her desire to foster children. Why would this sweet lady think being a victim was somehow her fault and would be counted against her? The sexual perpetrator often grooms his victim, and this causes the victim to believe it's not really wrong, or somehow that they are to blame because they think they have done something to attract the perpetrator. Let me just say it like this: if a child stands on a street corner with a sign that says, "please abuse me," it's still illegal, it's still abuse, and it is not the fault of the victim. I will also add that women are also perpetrators of abuse. In her book The Voice, singer Sandi Patty tells of how a trusted family friend, a woman, sexually abused her on multiple occasions as a young child.

Sexual abusers manipulate their victims into thinking they are playing some part in the abuse. It is often so confusing to a child to be used in this way and then told to keep it a secret. This is the lie we as victims of this type of abuse believe. Many of our disappointments are things that we take to our friends and family for help and encouragement, but not this one! The enemy will tell you that it's too awful and dark: "Better not let this secret out, or else you will be found out. They will know that you played a part in this, and it will ruin your life." Even the legal system can make it difficult to ask for help. Mandatory reporting can often stop us abuse victims in our tracks. My own child was reminded by her perpetrator that should she tell anyone, she would lose her family; that she would somehow be the one responsible for a family breaking up. My child, like many others, was given the message that she needed to hold the family together by not telling anyone about the abuse. What a terrible burden to put on a child. I don't have the answer for this. I am all for reporting abuse and prosecuting sexual offenders to the full extent of the law. I was, after all, a probation officer for a year... until I was let go for not being "smart" enough! But that is a different chapter.

I believe that there is power and healing that comes when we take this pain of abuse and use it to help other victims. How our family healed through this nightmare is a big reason why I wrote this book: to bring hope. I believe it is one thing for someone to use Romans 8:28 as a band-aid, and it's entirely different when someone such as myself has walked this walk. I fully believe that as awful as these disappointments are to our lives, there is hope! It is never God's will that we should continue to languish in the "what would have beens" of our lives. Disappointments are painful, but sharing them in the proper situation brings purpose to the pain. Shame will flourish in the dark, but when we bring it out into the open in the appropriate setting, it will help shame dissolve into purpose.

John 4:39 reminds us of why we share our stories. We don't tell our messy stories to get sympathy or attention. We tell our stories of disappointments to remind others what God has done and is doing in all of our lives; to let others know what God can do for them. In this story, a woman had met Jesus at a well, and she was a mess! She even waited until she knew others would have already gone to the well to draw her water. She did not want to deal with the shame and judgement she would surely have felt if others had seen her there. She'd had so many husbands that she avoided going to the well when most people did. Jesus didn't sugarcoat her sins. He told her that He knew about all of her husbands and that the man she was with right now was not her husband. He also let her know that He was the Messiah, the one who loved her and wanted to usher in healing to her heart.

John 4:39 (HCSB) says, "Now many Samaritans from that town believed in Him because of what the woman said." This is how we gain victory from our disappointments: we go and tell others what God has done with them. When we dig into this story a bit deeper, it is even more amazing. In the first century, women were devalued. Several first-century writings show that a man could divorce his wife for burning the bread! For a Rabi to even talk to a woman was very unusual. The only thing worse than being a woman in this time period was being a Samaritan woman! The Jews and Samaritans were not friends, to say the least! Jesus not only spoke to this woman, but she was the very first person He publicly told He was the Messiah to. He took this discarded, marginalized woman and made a missionary out of her!

In sharing our stories of abuse, we must be wise and discerning. I am not suggesting that you just drop it into daily conversation: "How is your day going? Great, did you know I was sexually abused?" I look at these hard disappointments as little hidden treasures to be shared wisely. Someone needs to hear your story, they really do! There is someone that you can bless and help bring about healing by letting them hear your story. You will also experience a power and a freedom by not holding the secret inside to be carried all by yourself. You can be real and honest, not fake and acting like everything is all okay if it is not. People need to know they are not alone, and with community, they can crawl out from under the heavy burden of being victimized by the horror of sexual abuse.

Yes, this "disappointment" is not beyond the healing hand of God. It's such a journey, and not an easy one. Sexual abuse involves your physical and emotional self; your sense of control and who is safe. It's such a complicated web of pain, but it can be healed, and yes... it does fall under the "Romans 8:28" category! Each time I share our story, each time a victim comes up to me to just be heard, I feel the oozing wound of sexual abuse healing into a scar.

Scars are wonderful reminders of how strong we are; of what did not take us down! The Bible says that Jesus took His scars to heaven. When His body rose from the grave, He had scars. In the book of John 20:20-25, Jesus invites "doubting Thomas" to put his whole hand in His side to feel the scars.

Have you ever thought about that? He could have had those removed and just had a resurrected body without them. I mean, if you can rise from the dead, I am pretty sure removing scars is not an issue. I believe they send us a powerful message of His love and triumph. I think Jesus kept His scars because He wanted us to know the price He paid for us and that He can relate to the scars we acquire in this life. If scars are good enough for the Lord, then I will gladly wear mine!

A word of advice about how to help someone who has been the victim of sexual abuse: listen, listen, listen! I was not good at this point. I wanted to fix, fix, fix! If someone is trying to tell you that they have been abused, let them get the details out. If someone is confiding to you about this, it is really an honor. Victims are fearful they will be dismissed or accused of lying. If someone is talking to you about it, then they must deem you someone they can trust, so listen to them.

It is very likely that the victim will start his or her conversation with "I need to tell you something but promise me you won't tell anyone." This can be tricky because of legal issues. If the victim is a child, reassure them that they are not going to be left alone to deal with this. Tell the child you want to keep them safe and that there are some other people whose job it is to help keep them safe. I think it is helpful to be honest. In my case, someone hotlined our family and then lied about it to me. I understand why the hotline was called, but I didn't appreciate the dishonesty. The hotline was found to be unsubstantiated as far as me being involved. To think that someone would even think I could allow my child to be abused was a painful issue I had to deal with and forgive.

When my daughter disclosed the abuse, I was very concerned mostly about getting a biblically based counselor. I think this was a mistake on my part. I wanted to give my family member hope that I believe is found only in God. I still fully believe this, but I should have also looked for a professional who was educated in sexual abuse. To slap some Bible verses on this topic is not effective. I know this sounds like heresy. I know God's Word is powerful, active, and can bring healing. I know that His Word never returns void. These are building blocks of my life. However, to not include the knowledge and psychology of sexual abuse, though, is not wise in my opinion. Most sexual abuse victims develop some temporary mental issues. These add pain to the already painful life of an abuse victim. When these go undiagnosed, it can delay healing. Post-traumatic stress disorder and borderline personality disorder are two common issues that can result from sexual abuse.

These are both issues that can be treated and dealt with by staying in therapy and looking to God for healing.

Look, I have a BS in Psychology, not a doctorate. I am not a mental health expert... or am I? I have lived with and experienced these disorders myself and watched them take a toll on my loved one. I have prayed, fasted, and quoted verse after verse. I am glad I did these things. I will continue to do them my entire life. They are powerful and healing. However, we are called to walk in wisdom. It says in the first chapter of James that if anyone lacks wisdom, let him ask God, who gives it to all generously. My understanding of this verse is that it is for anyone, believer and non-believer alike. This is one of those promises in God's word that says, "Hey, just ask and I will bring it on!"

I think to only seek biblical counseling for a sexual abuse survivor is not wise. I think the counselor should be both biblical and educated on the topic. Sexual abuse is evil and can cause damage to every area of a child. These victims are precious and strong and deserve all of the help they can get. I know in our story it would have been so much more helpful if I had known to look for a counselor who is experienced in the complex issues of sexual abuse. If you are an adult survivor of sexual abuse and have never found the healing you deserve, I would encourage you to seek out a trusted and educated therapist with a biblical perspective.

The last thing I will add to this list of how to help the survivor is don't put a time limit on when he or she should be "over it." Everyone is different; every journey is different. I know that we can't live in the past. I know that we need to practice radical acceptance of what has been and move on. This is so individual to each person. To tell someone they should be "over it by now" only brings another level of shame to a soul who is drowning in shame already.

I will end this chapter with some encouragement. My loved one is a survivor with lots of grit! They have endured a horrible wrong, but fought hard to learn how to deal with and recover from sexual abuse. To all of the sexual abuse survivors who are reading this book: stay at it! Don't ever believe that God can't turn your pain into a beautiful life! He indeed does make beauty from ashes! Read Isaiah 61:1-3. I have been able to use my being victimized by sexual abuse and being the mother of a victim of sexual abuse to help others heal, and in doing so, help me find some purpose to the pain.

The Romans 8:28 Truth: Survivors of sexual abuse are not alone. This is a problem many are dealing with, and help is available. This disappointment can be used to help others find healing and find that they are treasured and loved by a God who created them and gave them their worth.

CHAPTER 2

The Disappointment of Divorce

The Disappointment: A broken marriage.

The Disillusion: "I am unlovable, I am forever marked, I can no longer trust people."

Nobody walks down the aisle on the day of their wedding thinking it will someday end in a divorce. It says in the Old Testament book of Malachi that God "hates divorce." I think this is because He knows how much it destroys. I think it is because of how much He loves His children; He hates to see any of them ripped open by divorce. While God does not hate those of us who are divorced, he hates the concept of divorce.

I come from a long line of divorce in my family. My family of origin was a loving, caring one, but every marriage on one side of my family failed. Grandparents, parents, and siblings all dealt with the disappointment of divorce. When I dated in college and married my husband, I was determined to stop this family stronghold. I did lots of premarital counseling. I kept my purity until my wedding night. I married a strong Christian leader who was in campus ministry. I prayed and sought the Lord's guidance on who I should marry.

Despite all of these safeguards, my nearly seventeen-year marriage died in a courtroom one day as a judge pronounced our marriage dissolved. I was alone that day. My husband did not appear in court and my friend that was supposed to be there to support me... overslept. I remember walking out of the court into my car and driving to my soon-to-be repossessed home. My home that we had built was also being taken away. That home was to have been our forever house. We had put marks on wall to display the height of our children as they grew. It was the home I had dreamed of and prayed for.

It was clear that since my husband had been found out to have been sexually molesting a family member that he would not be able to keep his job and would eventually be going to prison. Our dream home house payment would be too much for me to keep up. I went from a stay-at-home mom in a 4500 square foot home to a single, unemployed, broken mom on food stamps with two hurting teens. It was mind-numbing, to say the least. I am forever grateful to my mom and brother helping us out with a new place to call our own. It was nice to be in a place that did not hold old memories. As it turned out, leaving our big house was a blessing in disguise. I am sure it was also better for my daughter to leave the house where she had endured such horrible abuse.

I wish mine was an isolated story that few of you can related to, but I know better. For many years, I have had the privilege of teaching in a singles class at my church. I've heard the stories both from both men and women who have gone through the heartbreak of divorce. One of my dear friends summarized it best when she said to me the other day, "I guess I will throw away all of my spices!" Oh, how I knew exactly what she meant. I used to be a wife; I had a home, entertained, cooked, and now... that has all been ripped away. I guess I will just "throw away my spices." I won't be needing them anymore. This may seem silly; I mean, you don't have to be married to bake, right?

To many newly divorced women, it appears to be all over. The purpose of being a wife—the ministry of being a Proverbs 31 wife—all over. Just this morning, I sat with a friend in church who had just been told her forty-nine-year marriage was ending. Her husband filed for divorce. Forty-nine years! Many men have a similar story. They were cheated on and told they were just "not enough" by the woman they loved, and now they get to see their kids on a visitation basis. I don't think they want to throw away their spices, but I'm sure they have a similar expression... "I guess I will throw away my power tools?" A man's house is his castle, after all, right?

There are so many in and out of the church who have endured a divorce. I remember going to my local Christian bookstore looking for some help in dealing with my divorce. I looked around at all the books but could not find anything on the topic. I finally went to the counter and asked the employee where the books on divorce were. He walked me over to the section of books about building a good marriage, pointed to the very bottom shelf of that section and showed me the one small section on the topic of divorce. Okay, first of all, we divorced people do not want to go anywhere near the "Happily Married" section of the bookstore, and second of all... the bottom shelf? Really? I remember thinking that was exactly how I felt: low and put on the bottom shelf. Today, many years later, I find that letting others know they are not alone, and that God can indeed walk them through this painful disappointment is the healing balm I needed to allow this wound to heal into a scar.

Having come from a broken home myself, I wanted my own children to never have to deal with divorced parents. Children of divorced parents are dealing with a family ripping apart. I wanted my children to know that my former in-laws were still family. I think when possible, this is so healthy. In most cases, as in mine, my in-laws had nothing to do with our marriage breaking up. As far as I was concerned, those were still my sisters-in-law, nieces, and nephews. It has been rewarding watching a whole generation of cousins love and celebrate birthdays together without having to take sides in a nasty divorce. I know this is not always possible, but when it happens, it makes for a beautiful story of grace and cousins who grow up to know each other and have a family legacy, despite the sadness of a marriage that ended in divorce.

When you see someone who has been through a divorce and is still standing, it gives hope and encourages others to not put a period where our loving God has put a semicolon. So many pages of the Bible are full of messy, embarrassing stories of broken people. When we share our stories or read the ones in the Bible, we see there are common threads, and these stories can bring hope. They are powerful. Don't let the lack of a ring on your left hand set your identity or tell you that you are less-than. When you are not so focused on being single, you can find the rewards in it, too. I love having a flexible schedule. I enjoy spending my money on what I want and not having to run it by a spouse. Both single and married life are full of rewards if we open our eyes to them.

God has a plan, and His plan is always good. The plans of the Lord are indeed good, but not always easy. I believe it's all part of the dance to keep us looking in the right direction for our peace and satisfaction. I understand that if you are not a follower of Christ, this may all seem silly, but if you think about it, most people believe someone created them, and what could be more valuable than learning how to draw closer to your Creator? The more you learn about God, the more you learn about how and why you were created, making for a more fulfilling life. In the Old Testament book of Jeremiah 29:11, God states He has good plans for us, plans for a hopeful future.

Today, as I write this, I am looking at seventeen years of being divorced and single. It's funny; my marriage lasted about the same amount of time. I have cried, fasted, tried online dating, and had several coffee dates, yet I have not been blessed at this point with a second marriage. I do have a funny story about a coffee date, though! It actually just popped into my head because right now, I am writing at the same coffee shop where said date happened!

My well-meaning daughter was tired of watching me wait for a spouse, so she took it into her own hands to make me a dating profile—without telling me! She is a great writer, so she made this poetic profile with a nice picture of me. Then, she waited for the fish to take the bait! Once she had what she thought was a reasonable match for a coffee date, she broke the news to me! I was horrified! She is an online dating professional. She told me I needed to kiss a few frogs before I found my prince...yada, yada. After looking at the guy's picture and reading his profile, I agreed to a coffee date.

I arrived early; it's a bad habit I have. I am always early for everything. Not long after, in walked the man who looked like the man my daughter had fixed me up with. He took one look at me and was way too excited! He sat down and just jumped right in. He spoke as if we had known each other all our lives. I guess that happens when you write your profile out. He knew my kids, my career, and my interests. It was all a bit too creepy for me. When he pulled out his phone and showed me that his new screen saver was my picture, that was it! I was out of there! I finally decided that if I couldn't trust a man I dated for several years and went through premarital counseling with, I wasn't about to trust a man who I just met online. Thus, this was the end of my online dating life!

I laugh at the story now. It's a funny one, but I know the heartbreak of lonely nights, wondering if you are going to be one of those people who grow old "alone." There is nothing funny about that. There is nothing wrong with online dating, but it's just not my cup of tea—or in this case, coffee.

I can say that God has given me peace about it either way, and I pray if you are reading this that you can find that peace. It came slowly by me learning that if God really loves me, if He really wants what's best for me and is able to do the impossible, then I can relax. Marriage is not a silver bullet. I know firsthand that it comes with its own set of issues. It is a good thing to find a godly spouse, but it takes work to make a lasting marriage. I am not afraid to do the work; I'm just letting God be in charge of this area in my life. I am content single; I will be content if I remarry. I think it is like Paul said in Philippians 4:13 (NKJV): "I can do all things through Christ who strengthens me." I can be single, or I can be married. Either way, I need the strength of Christ, and either way, because of Christ, I am going to be okay.

The older I get, the more I come to appreciate the fact that life is short. We have no guarantee of tomorrow. I pray that God gives me the grace to be thankful every day I wake up. I try not to spend my time bitter about the things that have not turned out the way I wanted in my life. We have feelings; God has made us with feelings, but when we put too much thought to disappointments of our lives, it robs us of the joys of today.

The Romans 8:28 Truth: God loves and heals those of us who have gone through a divorce. It does not disqualify us from the blessings God has in store for us.

CHAPTER 3

The Disappointment of Loss

The Disappointment: Loss of someone or something very dear to you.

The Disillusion: "I will hurt forever over this."

One of my objectives in writing this book was to be authentic. I realize there are many kinds of losses that I have not experienced in person, such as the loss of a pregnancy; the loss of a child. I don't want to write in theory, but out of experience. I do believe all losses have common threads, but I am not going to pretend I know how you feel if I have not experienced your loss. It is my prayer that whatever loss has brought you to, this chapter might be eased by reading it.

Loss: the word itself evokes a sad emotion—unless you are attending a weekly weigh-in at a weight loss meeting. As I write this, I am experiencing an unexpected devastating loss for me. I took my beloved dog Sam to the vet over the weekend and came home without him. My dog was my constant companion and my best friend, for sure. Let me give you an idea of how special he was. I have four beautiful grandchildren. My screensaver on my phone is my dog! He was rescued from a pound, but I often say he was the one who rescued me. His loss is felt deeply; since my children are grown, I live alone, and he was my companion. I never really came home to an empty house because Sam was always there waiting for me, tail wagging! When I worked as a foster care case manager, I often took him with me on visits to facilities. The children would light up as soon as they saw I had brought Sam along for our visit.

Animals are amazing therapists. They love unconditionally, forgive quickly, and are thankful for the small things. Sam was always waiting at the door, happy to see me. His companionship was such a blessing. Pets are like that. They are one of the nicest things ever created by God, in my opinion. A non-pet lover might say "Oh, it's just a dog." However, I would have to reply that Sam was "just" a dog no more than I am "just" a person. He filled a role in my life and in the lives of my family.

He will be very missed. When I looked into his eyes and said goodbye, I promised him I would rescue another dog someday when I was ready to open my heart again.

In some ways, it might be harder for us to lose a beloved pet than a person. We hope to see them again in heaven, but there is no direct scripture that says we will. I do believe God loves animals, and it is in His nature to care about them. There are scriptures that talk about animals in heaven, but nothing that directly says our pets will be there for us. Just for the record, I do believe I will see Sam again in Heaven. When I make that trip, he is the first one I want to see, right after Jesus! If we don't see our beloved pets in heaven, it must be because our need for them has been met by the Lord.

So, what do we do with grief from this type of loss? This can look like many things: loss of a marriage, a job, a dream, or a loved one. The past few days, I have just asked God to comfort me in my loss. I have found glimpses of comfort in being thankful for the wonderful memories and photos I have of Sam. My loss is still fresh and raw, and I have to allow God to tend to this gaping wound. When we experience loss, it may feel like we will never be happy again. Our feelings are a good indicator of how we feel, but they are not always a good indicator of truth. I once heard someone say, "Feel your feelings, don't feed them." I like this approach. If we don't allow ourselves to feel the grief, it is not healthy.

I cannot deny that my heart is aching for him. I cannot simply tell my heart to stop grieving. This approach would be unhealthy. If we continue to dwell on the loss and not look at the hope of a future in God's hands, that is also unhealthy. As sad as I am, I know that due to my past with God, I will not always hurt at this level over Sam's passing. I don't have to feel that God is near. It is nice when that happens, but it is not necessary for me to know He is near. Psalm 34:18 says that the Lord is near to the broken-hearted and saves those who are crushed in spirit. I believe this is true, even when my feelings say otherwise.

I have had a new loss come into my life since I last wrote in this chapter. I don't know how others write books. This is my first attempt at being a published author. I know the topics I want to write about, but I have skipped around in writing them. That is to say—I did not sit down and write chapter one and then chapter two and so on.

As I write this, I am currently on my way to attend a funeral of a loved one. The details are not mine to share and will remain private, but the lessons are universal. The death was a suicide. This has been so hard for the family for obvious reasons, but more so because the individual was such a loving, kind person. As someone who has experienced suicidal thoughts myself during my divorce, my heart aches for this person who felt like they had no other choice.

We can reach such a dark place that we feel we are not coming out of it. Suicide is the ultimate in hopelessness. Many well-meaning people say it is the ultimate in selfishness, but I would have to disagree. It is true that the act of suicide leaves a huge burden on the loved ones left behind. It causes a deep wound and leaves so many questions that can haunt the ones left behind. Why didn't they ask me for help? Why didn't I just know it was going to happen so I could have stepped in? Why was the gun in the house? Why didn't I get there in time to save them? Why were the pills in the house? These questions go on and on.

In most cases, the person taking their own life is fully convinced that their loved ones would be better off with them out of the way. I have dear friends I have known my entire adult life who lost a son to suicide. I have another friend who went to bed one night and woke up to a gunshot: a loved one had taken his life. In her book Fear Gone Wild, Kayla Stoecklein likens suicide to an accident. She lost her young husband to suicide. She says it's like a child drowning at a swimming party. There are loved ones around, but the child slips away and can't stay afloat any longer. The people at the party would have gladly jumped in to save the child had they seen it coming. In this way, it is an accident. They feel so broken; so much like they are such a burden to the family. This is not selfishness, its hopelessness.

As a believer with two beautiful children during my time of suicidal thoughts, many asked how I could possibly even think of leaving them alone. In my case, with their father now in prison, me taking my own life would have left them with no parents to raise them. As hard as it is to understand when someone is in that place of not wanting to go on, they are not thinking correctly or logically. I remember thinking that I was such an emotional burden to my kids and that they would be better off being raised by someone who was more emotionally healthy. The sadness and pain that someone is feeling at this point is hard to overestimate.

Thankfully, I did reach out for help and was given the help I needed. In my case, that was several weeks away from the situation in the hands of loving, capable, and caring counselors. God stepped in and provided the money to fly to the counseling, people to stay with my kids while I was away, and money to pay the bills while I was not working. There were many in my church and family who provided these things. To this day, I don't know who all paid for what, but ultimately it was God's provision, and I will be forever grateful. It is a reflection of a story in the Old Testament book of Exodus 17:8-13. In this story, the children of Israel were in a battle. When Moses would raise his hands, the Israelites would be winning, but if he lowered his hands, they would start to lose the battle. When Moses could no longer lift his hands on his own, Aaron and Hur would prop up his arms and bring a large rock for Moses to sit on. When I was no longer able to carry on myself, my friends and family came to "prop me up," if you will.

If you are at this point—that is, of not wanting to continue living, please reach out for help. Feeling suicidal thoughts is a lot like looking into a shattered mirror. The reflection you see is distorted, not the whole picture in reality. If you or someone you know is struggling with suicidal thoughts, there are people available twenty-four hours a day at the National Suicide Hotline, who you can call at 1-800-273-8255.

I do not know all of the details of my loved one's despair. I know they did have people who loved and cared deeply for them. Why I was able to ask for help and they did not seem to be at that place is a mystery to me, a painful one. I have a deep sense if sadness at the loss of my loved one. They were an amazing person, and I pray the legacy they left behind will be one of how they lived, not how they died.

There are many stories in the Bible of those who had no hope. Job is the one I think of most. There were others, such as Naomi and Moses, just to name a few. In the book of Job, we hear him ask these questions: "Why go on living when I have no hope?" (Job 6:11, GNT), "My days pass by without hope" (Job 7:6, GNT), "My days have passed; my plans have failed; my hope is gone" (Job 17:11, GNT), "Where is there any hope for me?" (Job 17:15, GNT). Job knew deep sorrow and emotional pain. He said, "I have no peace, no rest, and my troubles never end" (Job 3:26, GNT).

Job was tested like most of us will never be. He lost his family, his riches, his home, and his health. These losses were not as a result of him living a bad life. The Bible says he was a righteous man. He was tested to prove that he was faithful to God, not because of his blessings, but because he truly had a heart to love and obey God. I believe the book is there to teach us that bad things can happen to good people. The lessons in this book are many. In the end, God "blessed Job during the latter part of his life more than the former" (Job 42:12, ISV).

This is just another example of how life is not fair. I think we learn this faulty reasoning at childhood. How many of us stated, "That's not fair," to our parents when things didn't go the way we thought they should? I wish someone would have sat me aside at an early age and told me that life on this earth is beautiful and meaningful, yet not always what we would call "fair." There are many difficult things that have happened to me that I did not deserve, but there are also many great things that have happened to me that I didn't deserve either. When we let God be in charge of what is "fair" or "not fair," we can live with more peace and less worry.

This is not some wishful thinking. I have lived this out. That is why I have written this book. When these things came into my life, it was not my first reaction to just "grin and bear it." I knew God loved me, but these circumstances brought so much doubt into my heart. I could see no way out in many of these situations. The losses were staggering. The empathy it has given me, however, I am grateful for. It brings me purpose to the loss and pain. If we have to go through pain in this life, let's make good use of it.

I know someone who went to the dentist to have a painful tooth pulled. This person was afraid of the dentist and he asked to be put to sleep while the tooth was pulled. When he woke up, he found that the dentist had pulled the wrong tooth! That is what I called wasted pain! The story has always stuck with me because I don't want to waste any pain I have to go through. If we have to go through pain, and Jesus said that it's part of all of our journeys, then make it count for something good and useful.

CHAPTER 4

The Disappointment of Physical Pain or Illness

The Disappointment: Physical pain or illness that keeps you from living life the way you want.

The Disillusion: "The pain will keep me from living a fulfilling life."

Today is Sunday, and I have places to be. I should have arrived at church by 9:00 a.m. to sing in our morning service. I needed to be in church to give my elderly mom a ride home. I just really needed to be in church, because today, I am discouraged due to my chronic back pain. I have degenerative back disease. Oddly, one of the reasons I started a cleaning business was to stay active and keep my back moving. There are days when I overdo it with working and picking up my little bundles of joy (grandkids). Today, my back said, "No more! We are done!" I have been in bed all day, taken pain medication, turned my phone off, and ordered delivery because I needed to get groceries today and have no food!

I just celebrated my fifty-seventh birthday a few days ago. When back pain days keep me in bed, my mind veers off into a not-so-happy place. *What if I have to stop working? What if I can't pay my bills? What if I can't be as active as I want to be?* As I lay in bed this morning thinking of all the people who depend on me to clean their houses, I am disappointed that this day will be a "waste."

Chronic pain can leave us feeling pretty hopeless. It is all-consuming and is a difficult thing to get your mind off of. Pain demands all of our energy, and it is hard to focus on much else. It was then that it hit me: I should include this as a chapter in my book. I am always saying, "Don't waste your pain."

Let's return back to our main verse, Romans 8:28 (HCSB): "We know that all things work together for the good of those who love God: those who are called according to His purpose." The question I ask is how can illness and physical pain be good in any way? I am so quick to see the bad. For starters, it hurts! Back pain or chronic pain of any kind is, well... painful. An illness can just stop me in my tracks. When I am in physical pain, it is hard to focus on much else. It is hard to take care of my daily needs. I am sure I don't need to go on about this obvious point. If I can take my pain to God in prayer and ask Him to not only take my pain away but show me how to use it for the good talked about in the Bible verse, then I am on to something.

How many of us have heard stories of people in the hospital, in pain, who somehow managed to share the love of Christ with others in the same hospital? I know friends who have said the time they were flat on their backs was the most precious time they had with God. Sometimes God has to slow us down to get our attention and to remind us that all we have, including our health comes from His hand.

I am not saying God causes all illness or pain. The fact is, we live in a fallen world for the time being. Sickness and pain are a result of the fall. Not the "fall" like pretty leaves falling, I mean the fall, like the "Eve ate the apple" kind of thing. Many times, we need this pain to gain perspective that this life is a precious but temporary situation. For the Christian, this is not our final destination, and maybe we need to be reminded of that to get a little homesick. This is not some ego-driven God we serve, but one who loves to provide for His children in ways that are not of this world. He has the power to remove the pain, but He often chooses to carry us through it for higher reasons. I have had other days with severe pain, and I have fully relied on God to get me out of bed and going. The comfort and strength He has given me on those days is amazing. I know that He has heard my prayer and carried me through the day.

These days of knowing that God walked me through my pain and allowed me to carry out my workday build my faith. Faith is like a muscle: we need to exercise it to build it up. Then what about the days like today? I asked God to help me get up and remove my pain or just give me the strength to work through it, but... crickets! Nothing! I'm here in bed with the old heating pad. These days are no less an answer to prayer, though. I have walked with the Lord now long enough to know He has a purpose, and He cares.

In Psalm 46:10, it states that we need to be still and know that He is God. The original meaning of the phrase "be still" is "to let go." Let go and know that He is God. In other words, when it doesn't go as we have planned, let go of the need to control everything and remember that He is good and He is in control. Much of this kind of thinking is just a simple choice; not an easy choice always, but a simple one. If I trust Him and I look back at my history with God, I can then let go and let Him be my God. I want to be clear: happiness is a choice, but our feelings are not always so easy to fall in line. You make the choice to trust God through the pain, and sometimes your feelings don't always agree.

You still may be upset, mad and angry, but push on through by the grace of God. Tell Him how you feel and trust Him despite those feelings.

The Bible talks about the mighty apostle Paul having some kind of physical ailment in his body. In 2 Corinthians 12:7, it says that a thorn in the flesh was given to Paul so he would not exalt himself. God knew that Paul was to be given some amazing revelations and could easily have gotten a big head over his spiritual knowledge. Scripture states that he asked God to remove this pain in his body three times! God dearly loved Paul, just as He dearly loves us, yet God knew that taking away this thorn would not be the best thing for Paul and for the kingdom. God did not ignore his prayers; instead, He said that His grace would be enough and would be sufficient.

Some days, my back pain makes is difficult to just get out of bed. On these days, my focus is on God so much more. I have a cleaning business, and I fully rely on God to give me the strength to go to work. God has provided medication for me and I take it, but the pain is a reminder of sorts that I need to allow God, to trust that God will carry me through my day, pain and all. It keeps me dependent on Him, and that is the place I want to live my life, strangely enough. I would much rather live life with the power of God than in my own limited capabilities.

I know precious saints who are in severe pain from accidents, diseases, and aging. Many of these people just amaze me by the smiles on their faces and the joy in their hearts. I know attitude goes a long way in re setting our minds. When the pain you bear is miserable and you are not sure you see any light at the end of the tunnel, that is a difficult burden, for sure. My physical pain comes and goes, and I can't say that I have had prolonged periods of constant stay-in-bed pain.

I don't want to seem trite about severe pain, yet I still believe there has to be some purpose in it. I think the Bible verse that brings me comfort in physical pain is the one that talks about how God's mercies are new every morning. This means that tomorrow morning when I get up, I don't have to use my leftover mercies from yesterday. His strength and mercy to deal with my pain is a brand-new dose each morning. This scripture is found in the Old Testament in the book of Lamentations 3:22-23. This book is full of sorrow and lamenting, not so much for physical pain, but for the spiritual and emotional kind. The author of this book was watching his beloved people face consequences for sinful behavior, and it broke his heart. Despite watching his people suffer, the writer of Lamentations still remembers that his hope is in God and that each new day brings new mercies to deal with our sufferings. I have found that needing God means I get to know God in a deeper way, and it gives me strength for my journey.

CHAPTER 5

The Disappointment of Mental Illness

The Disappointment: Mental illness.

The Disillusion: "I am forever damaged and messed up."

I have much respect for Pastor Rick Warren and his wife Kay. They have championed the cause of mental illness in the church the last several years. They know the deep pain of this issue, as they lost a precious young adult son to suicide. Rick often reminds the church at large that to take a pill for a heart condition is not considered shameful. If you heart does not work, or your blood sugar is off, you can take a pill to assist those organs. If, however your brain is not working or chemicals are off in that part of the body, taking a pill brings shame to many in church circles. The brain is, after all, an organ of our body. If we have high blood sugar, we can be told to take a pill and get some exercise. Why, then, when our brain is out of balance can we not take a pill and also get some exercise? I am not saying that it is the complete answer, but I feel many Christians who suffer from mental illness think using this protocol to treat mental illness somehow makes them less of a Christian. There is such a stigma towards mental illness, and this type of thinking just adds to the problem.

The Lord Jesus is our chief physician. As believers in Christ, we look to God to ask for health and healing. We should pray and take care of our bodies to the best of our abilities. When medication is called for by a trusted and educated doctor, we should follow the orders just like we would if we had an ear infection or some other illness. I believe most people today would walk out of a psychological evaluation diagnosed with some sort of mental illness. Goodness, this world we live in is full of anxiety and can cause fear in the strongest of people. We as the church should love and hold up those suffering from a mental illness, not cause them more pain by shaming them for not having enough faith to just "snap out of it!"

Several years ago, I was diagnosed with generalized anxiety disorder, or GAD. I would startle very easily if I heard a loud noise. I had some legitimate concerns in my life, but the level of anxiety they were causing me was off the chart! I wanted to try to just deal with it by getting more exercise and going to see a good counselor. These are great for anxiety. However, one of the stressors I was having was due to financial pressure, so the therapy part was not going to happen without paying for it. My doctor told me that she wanted to try a low dose of medication to assist the chemicals in my brain to be able to do their job and help with anxiety. She also suggested talking to friends and family and exercise. This approach has helped me to live a better quality of life, and I don't suffer as much with anxious thoughts. The key is to get with a good doctor and discuss your options.

I also worked as a case manager for several years with severely mentally disabled adults. These precious ones were suffering so much that they had to be placed in a locked facility and assigned a case manager to help them cope with persistent mental illnesses. The severity varied. Some of my clients had bipolar disorder. This is where you have extreme mood swings. When you are happy, you are off-the-charts happy. When you are down, it is a deep dive to despair. It can be difficult to get these patients to take their medication because they did not want to give up the "high" that came with the manic episodes that gave them a feeling of euphoria. Some had schizophrenia, some had depression, and some had various other disorders. I would visit them weekly and try to assist them in making their quality of life better. This was done in various ways. Sometimes we went out for a drive. Sometimes we went over what their individual medications looked like with flash cards. This gave these individuals a sense of hope and some control to their lives. They were given their medications by a medical tech, but by knowing what medications they were on, they could easily spot a mistake if given the wrong medication. I would often take some of them to mental health court if they were dealing with the law.

Mental illness has no favorites! I have worked with clients who had college degrees, those who were successful professionals, and those who were homeless. It was an honor to be able to help these precious ones. One year for Christmas, I asked the facility what we could do to bring some holiday cheer to those living in this facility. She said the residents of this facility never got to enjoy home cooking, and they would be thrilled to get some homemade desserts. I got my family and some friends from my church to start baking! We ended up with around twenty-five pies and cakes to deliver to the facility. My friend Stephanie plays the piano, so we brought along a keyboard. My oldest granddaughter loves the spotlight, so she was happy to have a captive audience. We sang Christmas carols and she danced and sang her heart out!

There are examples of mental illness in scripture. King David was up one minute and down another. He was considered "a man after God's own heart," yet also committed murder and adultery. His own family was a mess. He had a daughter who was raped by her half-brother Amnon. This story is in 2 Samuel 13. His own son Absolom tried to overthrow David and take over his kingdom. My guess is he would have been told he had bipolar disorder.

Elijah would surely have been recognized to have suicidal thoughts and been diagnosed with manic depressive disorder! After a huge victory on Mt. Carmel, he ran away in fear, hid, and asked God take his life! In 1 Kings 19, we see this mighty man of God sitting under a tree, telling God that he has had enough and to just let him die! Have you ever been there? Just enough, already—enough struggle, enough failure and disappointment. I certainly have been there. God heard Elijah, and He cared for and loved the prophet. He listened to him and sent him what he needed to get on with his life.

Job is another example of someone who faced depression. He lost his children, his possessions, and his health. He was surely depressed as any one of us would be dealing with such staggering losses. His story is found in the Old Testament book of Job. However, God was near and delivered him. The Bible says, "The Lord

blessed the latter end of Job more than his beginning"
(Job 42:12, KJV). In the end, Job found the good and the
meaning and purpose of his suffering and went on to
lead a full and wonderful life.

If you or someone you know is struggling with
mental illness, you are certainly not alone. The National
Alliance on Mental Illness (NAMI) website lists 300 famous people who also struggled or are currently struggling with these issues. I won't list all 300 of them, but I
have pulled some out of the list to show you:

- Paula Deen: agoraphobia and panic attacks
- Mel Gibson: bipolar disorder
- Ludwig van Beethoven: bipolar disorder
- Winston Churchill: bipolar disorder; dyslexia
- Buzz Aldrin: clinical depression
- Dolly Parton: clinical depression
- Harrison Ford: clinical depression
- Pablo Picasso: clinical depression
- Donny Osmond: clinical depression; social
  phobia
- Danny Glover: learning disability
- Abraham Lincoln: severe clinical depression

As we can see from this list, mental illness can affect
all classes and ages of people. We can also see by this
list that these were famous people who were successful

in their own lives. Mental illness can be dealt with and overcome with help. It also gives us a chance to gain a greater perspective for those who struggle with these illnesses.

CHAPTER 6

The Disappointment of Unemployment

The Disappointment: A job loss.

The Disillusion: "I am a loser; a failure."

I would say that I have a strong work ethic. In any job I have had, I try my best and pray for God to give me wisdom and diligence. When I went through my divorce, I found myself looking for a full-time job in a town that runs on tourism. I have a BS in Psychology and discovered quickly there was not much available in my area for my degree. After my youngest went on to college, I moved to a town that offered more in the way of job opportunities. I went through so many different jobs. Some were not a good fit for my abilities, but I took them out of desperation. Others were working for small nonprofits who had bad leadership, poor training, and no human resources departments.

I live in the state of Missouri. Missouri is what is called an "at will" state. This means an employer can let you go when they feel like it. They might have to end up paying unemployment, but they can let a worker go at will. I enjoyed a few years working at a local college until the college closed and I was once again unemployed. As a probation officer, I was told one day after almost a year with no write ups that I "just wasn't catching on quick enough." As a children's division worker, I spent lots of time on the road and enjoyed it, but as most of these jobs go, I burned out after two years. Job failure after job failure just piled on the self-doubt and frustration. As a single woman who has the only income in the home, a job is a must.

I think the disappointment came from wondering why God was not helping me or leading me in this area. I had been diagnosed with a learning disability when I was very young. As it turns out, I learn much better by hearing something than by reading it. This was frustrating when I needed to learn a new software system or other skills on a new job. The feelings of rejection also piled up. I can honestly say that this area was as frustrating and disappointing as the other topics in this book. The financial stress and the sense of not belonging anywhere in the job field can be very difficult.

There are many other desires that we want but don't necessarily need. A job, however, is a must!

There were many days I did not walk through this valley well. I was filled with self-doubt and a false belief that I had missed my purpose somewhere along the way and would have to settle for a second-rate life. As a believer in Christ, I know this was not God's will for my life, and if you find yourself in the same boat, it's not His will for your life either! Often when we are let go of a job, we are afraid and seem to take the first thing we can find. This is such a walk of faith. On the one hand, we have bills piling up and we can see the financial disaster up ahead if we don't start bringing in some income.

I have found in my life that any decision I make out of fear is usually not a good one. Fear tells us that we had better look out for ourselves, because no one else is going to. This is especially true if someone has been fired for no good reason. I know on some level, I felt that God had not watched out for me. I was doing my best and I still lost jobs. We have to be responsible and not expect others to pay our bills, yet we should also be selective in taking on a new job. If we can take an honest look at why we lost a job or why we quit a job, it will help us make a wise decision in looking for a new job.

Today, I am picking up this chapter after several weeks of not writing. Wow, what a difference a couple of weeks can make in our lives. As of today, our world is reeling under the pandemic of the COVID-19 virus. There are so many around the world dying, sick, lonely, and yes, out of work! As a self-employed worker, I was relieved to hear the government is providing unemployment for the self-employed during this time. I am considered an essential worker but because I am caring for my elderly mother and helping to homeschool my granddaughter; I made the decision to close my business for now during this time. I don't want to risk bringing home the virus to my mom, and all of my clients are now working from home due to the closure of so many businesses.

This is such a dark time for all of us, but as the Bible verse I keep touting in the book says, all things will be worked out for the good! I am finding it crazy that my stable friends who have never before attempted to navigate the unemployment website are now calling me for help! I had to smile! I have had lots of experience with the unemployment process, and it has been a blessing for those who have no clue how the thing works. I never though anything good would come of my job struggles. It is nice to see God using such a painful time in my past to help others today in my present. If you are unemployed, try to remember that your identity is not found in your work. You are valuable because God created you in His image, and He does have a purpose for your life.

I finally took inventory of all my job losses and things I enjoy doing. I think for me, social work had become so unproductive. I never really got to see much good for all the work I was pouring into the field. Social workers are very hard workers and so helpful for our society. They are sadly underpaid and underappreciated in many areas.

When I decided to start a cleaning business, it was a risk. Would I get enough clients? Would I be good at it? I am now on year four of my business. I can tell you that it has been one of the best decisions of my life! I enjoy the productivity of seeing my work result in a clean house for my clients, and I enjoy helping people. I love being my own boss, taking off when I need to, and not sweating the thought of having to ask my boss for time off to go to an appointment! It has been such a surprise blessing for me. I would have never had the guts to do this had I not had so many struggles in the job area. I had to smile when this Christmastime I received $550.00 in Christmas tips from my clients! I was humbled and thankful. The most I received in the way of a Christmas bonus in my social work days was usually a frozen turkey!

Although there is no story in the Bible about unemployment per say, I find the book of Ruth to hold the same principals. Let's take a look. When the book opens, we find a husband, Elimelek, and his wife, Naomi. They have two sons and are living in a land far from their homeland due to a famine. The sons both have taken wives in this foreign land. The short version is that after some time, Naomi's husband and both of her sons die. She is left in a foreign land with two daughters in laws and no children or grandchildren. In other words, she has no heir. This is a terrible disappointment, because in this culture, women who were left with no man to look after them were just destined to live in poverty. They could not own or buy land and they could not go out and earn a living.

Naomi appears to be a follower of God based on Ruth 1:20, which we will look at in a minute. When it is clear that Naomi will not be able to sustain her life in the foreign land, she sets off to return to Moab, her homeland. She tells her daughters-in-law to stay behind and try and find new husbands to be able to live and start a family with. In all of this loss and grief, we see her daughter-in-law Ruth. Ruth refuses to leave her mother-in-law and begs her to let her journey back to Moab with her. Ruth knows nothing of Moab and is not from the same culture, yet her love and devotion to her mother-in-law is what is most important to her. The two women set out on this journey back to Moab. We usually don't consider this when reading this passage, but this was a dangerous task. Two women traveling alone would have been considered risky at best.

Let's pick up the story in Ruth 1:19-20, when the two women went on until they came to Bethlehem. When they arrived in Bethlehem, the whole town was stirred because of them, and the women exclaimed, "Can this be Naomi?" "Don't call me Naomi," she told them. "Call me Mara, because the Almighty has made my life very bitter. I went away full, but the Lord has brought me back empty. Why call me Naomi? The Lord has afflicted me, the Almighty has brought misfortune upon me."

I think this is how some of us must feel when our prayers for a job seem to go unanswered. Just as God was getting ready to use this misfortune for the good in Naomi and Ruth's lives, He also can and will use our job losses for our good if we hang in there. At the end of the book of Ruth, we see Naomi holding her new grandbaby boy, and Ruth is now married to a good guy! I once heard someone say that when you are waiting for a husband, don't settle for "bozo" when you can have Boaz!

The Romans 8:28 lesson here is to be patient and wise and wait for God to bring about a good ending to your unemployment chapter.

CHAPTER 7

Let's Get Real!

One of my favorite Christian artists is Matthew West. He has many songs, but one of his new ones is my favorite. The name of the song is "Truth Be Told." It speaks of how we all feel like we need to have it all together in Christian circles. One of the lines in the song says: "Truth be told, the truth is rarely told."

This brings me to the point of this chapter: being real and honest. This not only means being honest with others, but being honest with God. Being honest with prayer, honest prayer, is powerful. It can feel strange to be gut-level honest with the God of the universe because He is so holy, and we should have a reverence for Him. There are many scriptures that also speak to the desire of God's heart for His children to be honest with Him. King David wrote many of the Psalms and he had a relationship with God that was honest and real. In Psalm 51:8, David talks to God and asks him to cleanse him and restore the bones that God himself has broken. The twenty-third Psalm is a famous one. In it, David states that even though we walk through the valley of the shadow of death, we will fear no evil because God is with us. Think about what that means. We walk through the valley; we don't camp out there. As we walk through the valley, our all-knowing, all-powerful God walks right there beside us. If you think about this further, we see that in order to even have a shadow, we need light. God is that light walking through the valley of death with us and casting that shadow.

In both of these Psalms, David does not skirt around the pain he is feeling. He states that God has caused the crushing pain as a result of David's sins. He states that he is walking through the valley of death. Honest prayer is not a denial of facts or feelings. God does not want us to be fake or phony with him. God knows it all anyway. He wants us to come to Him, knowing He is holy and righteous, and to just be real with Him in our praying.

My son has recently been in a health battle. We found out yesterday that they are testing him now for leukemia and lymphoma. My son is thirty-three years old, healthy, and on top of the world. He has a beautiful wife and three healthy children. His career is rewarding to him, and he has a lot of success in his field. The last few weeks have been sleepless ones for most of us that love Jordan. I have been honest with God about my fears of losing him or watching him go through a painful diagnosis. I have "reminded" God about what a great father and husband Jordan has been and how he honors and loves God. His wife and kids need him; I need him. In crying out to God, I have found so much comfort and peace. I am convinced that should we be entering into a cancer battle; we are armored up as a family, and our God will fight right alongside us.

Is this what I want? Of course not! I will pass on the opportunity to show that I can keep my faith while watching my son deal with cancer. I am praying the blood tests show some virus or some other easy-to-heal-from illness. I will pray that I will watch Jordan grow old and have grandchildren of his own. However, should we get bad news of the blood test, we would not be the first! We will not shrink back from the Lord, but bury our heads in His chest and cry out for His love and mercy. Jordan is such a gift to me, and I have been so blessed to get to be his mom. His sister always teases him that he is such a momma's boy, and I tell her, "You better believe it!"

The principle is this: disappointment + honest prayer = hope in God's plans. There are so many saints in the Bible who cried out in honest prayer. Elijah cried out to end his life. Joseph cried out in pain at the rejection of his family. Hannah had words with God about being childless. Jesus cried in the garden for God to "let this cup pass," yet He resigned Himself to accept the Father's will as the best. David cried out for forgiveness.

Peter rebuked Jesus, and Job grieved at the loss of his children and possessions. There is a pattern here, and I believe God is telling us to be authentic and truthful with each other and with Him. This honesty will bring us strength in our battles and peace in our journey.

CHAPTER 8

Recycle It!

I have a sweet family member who comes to me for advice. I am constantly giving her the same reply: "Put your hope in God!" She gets tired of hearing this and will often say to me, "How can you say that after all you have been through?" I love her dearly and tell her that if I had a better answer, I would have surely given it to her by now. How can I not put my hope in God? If it were not for Him, I would have been taken out by all of the disappointments I have written about in this book. We simply just can't see all that He is up to. He is not on our timetable, and He wants the best for us.

Trouble and disappointments are not new, as we have seen in this book. We also know lots of people who are walking through hard times right now, and we will meet lots of people in our future who will need our encouragement as they navigate difficult waters. This has been a difficult year for everyone with the COVID-19 pandemic. We have lost loved ones and friends; lost the ability to do some of the things we have always been able to do freely. 2020 has been a disappointing year. I myself had to drop my elderly mother off at the emergency room after a fall and was not able to go into the hospital and sit with her. I know friends who have had parents shut up in nursing homes with dementia during the pandemic and these individuals have no idea why their loved ones don't come visit anymore. Seniors have lost graduation ceremonies, proms, and other significant special events. I have a friend who got married during this time and was not able to have her friends and family attend the wedding. The same has held true for funerals attended by only a few family members. These events are just a few of the disappointments we as a world have gone through this year, yet these dark days have also brought families back to the dinner table together, and more pets have been adopted from shelters bringing joy into the home. We have had to opportunity to stop and check our priorities and perspectives. This past year at Thanksgiving, it seems our family was more thankful for the little things and appreciated the get-together we might sometimes take for granted.

I used to imagine God as a parent at a playground watching over His children like we so often see in our daily lives. Picture a city playground or even a school playground. The parents or teachers are all there nearby, watching the kids. If a child falls or gets hurt, a loving parent or teacher will come over and pick up the child and help give comfort. I have learned that God is not only like that, but He is actually right beside me—right there, not watching from a distance. He will catch and has caught me many times when I have fallen. He is near. He stays so much closer than we imagine. The verse that says that God is near to the brokenhearted and saves those who are crushed in spirit is found is Psalm 34:18.

The more I walk with God, the more I believe my need of Him is vital and pleasing to Him. God designed us to need Him not only for our salvation, but for the longings of our hearts. I know that each disappointment I have gone through has led me closer to God. On the surface, my flesh screams, "Well, that looks nice on a greeting card, but I need [fill in the blank]." Things such as money to pay bills, the scale to stop going up, a boyfriend, a husband, a job, a car that works. I have wanted and needed some or all of these things. I need a job to pay my bills; I need a car to get to work. This is true, but more than this, I have come to learn that what I ultimately need is to trust my God to supply all of my needs.

Philippians 4:19 is a popular verse for many. It encourages us that God will supply all of our needs according to His riches in glory in Christ Jesus. I love this for many reasons. I can rest assure that all my needs will be met. This does not say all my wants, though He meets many of these, also. It says that God meets our needs, but not with His leftovers. He meets our needs with His very best riches in glory in His son Jesus. When I try to fill these needs on my own, it may work, but I miss the best that God has for me. I may be able to find a job, but by not trusting and seeking God to guide me in the search, I may end up with a job that is not the best fit for me. I may be able to buy a car, yet if I realize that God owns it all and ask for His best for me, I believe I end up with a better car.

God is not a slot machine; He is not a genie in a bottle. We don't just go to God when we need things. We stay in a relationship with Him on a daily basis. Only then can we truly know what we really need and how much He longs to help us with our needs and some of our wants, too.

Afterword

It has been one of the joys of my life to write this book. I have had many doubts as to if I could really write and publish a book. I have put the manuscript down several times and kept having the nudge to finish it. God has been so patient and kind with me to give me the words to write and the ability to publish! I am a new author, so I have no idea how this book will sell. My heart's desire and belief are that someone out there needs to have this book to know they can be disappointed without being disillusioned.

I want to close with some powerful scriptures, but before I share those, I want to share a quote from a great writer. In his book Dream Big, Bob Goff says, "What you need to really believe in your gut is that, in God's economy, nothing is ever wasted. Not your pain, nor your disappointments, not your setbacks. These are your tools. They can be used later as a recipe for your best work. Quit throwing the batter away."

Helpful Scripture

Consider it pure joy, my brothers, when you face trials of many kinds. Because you know that the testing of your faith produces perseverance. Let perseverance finish its work so that you may be mature and complete, not lacking anything.

James 1:2-4 (NIV)

We are assured and know that (God being a partner in their labor) all things work together and are (fitting into a plan) for good to and for those who love God and are called according to (His) design and purpose.

Romans 8:28 (AMP)

Peace I leave with you; my peace I give you. I do not give to you as the world gives. Do not let your hearts be troubled and do not be afraid.

John 14:26-27 (NIV)

I waited patiently for the Lord, he turned to me and heard my cry.

Psalm 40:1 (NIV)

But I trust in you Lord; I say, my times are in your hands.

Psalm 31:14 (NIV)

As cheesy as it sounds, turn your mess into your message, go from bitter to better, and make your test your testimony!

Endorsement

"Deb's life echoes the Psalmist's words, "Come and listen, all you who fear God; let me tell you what He has done for me." (Psalm 66:16). Her story is a testimony of God's grace and a beautiful encouragement to not let disappointments turn to disillusionment.

—Paula Voris , MSW
Minister of Connections
Second Baptist Church
Springfield MO

CPSIA information can be obtained
at www.ICGtesting.com
Printed in the USA
LVHW031334130721
692557LV00010B/1028